MW01388784

Lessons At The Cross

Compiled by
Michael Burdette

Lessons At The Cross

Another Fine Offering From
~ The Fire Press ~

ISBN: 0-9655098-3-4
Copyright 2004 by Mike Burdette

Published by **Level 10 Publications**
1860 Pope Creek Road
Wildwood, Georgia 30757

Printed in the United States of America. All rights reserved under International Copyright Law. Contents and/or cover may not be reproduced in whole or in part in any form without the express written consent of the Publisher.

Dedication

I would like to dedicate this book to four people. The first two are my parents, who planted the seeds that needed to be watered in me. Next, my wife who has always supported me and loved me even when I didn't deserve either. Last, I would like to make a special dedication to Randy McNeely, who led me to Christ. Randy left this earth on January 31, 1999, and there hasn't been a day I don't think of him. But I look forward to seeing him again in God's kingdom.

On November 2, 1997, my life changed. I became a Christian, I'm proud to say. People ask me, "What were you before?" and I always say, "I don't know, but you wouldn't have liked me much."

What you just read is a direct quote that I make many times a month. No, I don't like repeating myself. This quote is made in public to hundreds of people. I know what you're thinking: He must be a minister. No, but I do have a ministry. The fact is that I am actually a public speaker and sales trainer, primarily for the automobile industry. My job is what I do but not who I am. However, it provides me a chance to be a faithful witness for the Lord. This leads me to the reason for this book. I work for a man by the name of Paul Cummings whose grandfather inspired Paul to write a book entitled *Lessons At The Fence Post*.

Since that Sunday in November of 1997, when I accepted the Lord as my savior, I have tried to be a sponge for the Lord's lessons. Not just through the Bible, but through other people's testimonies and nationally known publications.

Inspired by *Lessons At The Fence Post*, I have compiled Biblical-based lessons that have impacted me. My hope and prayer are that they will also touch a place in your heart. Inspired by the greatest teacher of them all, Jesus Christ, I humbly bring you *Lessons At The Cross*.

- Mike Burdette

Lessons At The Cross

~ Lessons At The Cross ~

If You Put God First ... You Will Never Come In Second.

– Compiled by Michael Burdette

You Will Never Forgive More Than You Already Have Been Forgiven.

– Compiled by Michael Burdette

~ Lessons At The Cross ~

~ Lessons At The Cross ~

**Born Once ... Die Twice ...
Born Twice ... Die Once.**

– Compiled by Michael Burdette

S top
I t
N ow

Compiled by Michael Burdette

~ Lessons At The Cross ~

~ Lessons At The Cross ~

**Worry Is The Interest Paid
On Trouble Before It's Due ...
Let The Lord Hold The Note.**

– Compiled by Michael Burdette

I Am Blessed And Highly Favored.

– Compiled by Michael Burdette

~ Lessons At The Cross ~

True Freedom Rings Through God's Grace.

– Compiled by Michael Burdette

Don't Plan To Repent At The 11th Hour ... You Might Die At 10:30 ...

– Compiled by Michael Burdette

~ Lessons At The Cross ~

E dging
G od
O ut

— Compiled by Michael Burdette

God Can Mend A Broken Heart ... But You Have To Give Him All The Pieces.

– Compiled by Michael Burdette

~ Lessons At The Cross ~

~ Lessons At The Cross ~

**Life Is Change ...
Growth Is Optional.**

– Compiled by Michael Burdette

Sin Adds To Your Trouble ... Subtracts From Your Energy ... And Multiplies Your Difficulties. You Do The Math.

– Compiled by Michael Burdette

~ Lessons At The Cross ~

~ Lessons At The Cross ~

Grow In The Lord. When You're Green, You're Growing ... When You're Ripe, You're Rotten.

– Compiled by Michael Burdette

Because God's Grace Paid The Price Once ... You Can Receive The Value Every Day.

– Compiled by Michael Burdette

~ Lessons At The Cross ~

~ Lessons At The Cross ~

**When Life Knocks You Down,
Make Sure You Land On
Your Back ...
Because If You Can Look Up,
You Can Get Up.**

– Compiled by Michael Burdette

Pulling Yourself Up By Your Bootstraps Begins By Bending Your Knees.

– Compiled by Michael Burdette

~ Lessons At The Cross ~

~ Lessons At The Cross ~

**You May Lose Everything ...
But You Will Never Lose
Your Salvation.**

– Compiled by Michael Burdette

If God Is Your Co-Pilot ...
Try Switching Seats.

– Compiled by Michael Burdette

~ Lessons At The Cross ~

~ Lessons At The Cross ~

God's Love ... Every Day ... Every Time ... Without Fail ... No Exceptions.

– Compiled by Michael Burdette

Your 911 Emergency Operator's Name Is Jesus ... Call Anytime.

– Compiled by Michael Burdette

~ Lessons At The Cross ~

~ Lessons At The Cross ~

When God Closes A Door ... He Will Open A Window ... When Both Window and Door Are Shut, Jesus Is Your Escape Hatch.

– Compiled by Michael Burdette

When Lifting Your Problems Off Your Chest ... Use God As Your Spotter.

– Compiled by Michael Burdette

~ Lessons At The Cross ~

~ Lessons At The Cross ~

WWJD (What Would Jesus Do)? ... First, Know WHDD (What He Did Do).

– Compiled by Michael Burdette

**Motivation Lasts A
Short Time ...
Education Lasts A Lifetime ...
Salvation Knows No Time.**

– Compiled by Michael Burdette

~ Lessons At The Cross ~

Take Stock In God ... He Will Never Cook The Books.

– Compiled by Michael Burdette

B elievers'
I nstructions
B efore
L eaving
E arth

– Compiled by Michael Burdette

~ Lessons At The Cross ~

The Prize Fighter Doesn't Worry About Getting Knocked Down ... He Worries About Not Getting Up. God Will Never Count You Out.

– Compiled by Michael Burdette

Instead Of Thinking 'I Am Great,' Give Glory To The Great I Am.

– Compiled by Michael Burdette

~ Lessons At The Cross ~

I May Not Know What Tomorrow Holds ... But I Know Who Holds Tomorrow.

– Compiled by Michael Burdette

G od
R eceiving
A ll
C hrist
E mpowered

– Compiled by Michael Burdette

~ Lessons At The Cross ~

~ Lessons At The Cross ~

God Doesn't Promise Smooth Sailing, But He Does Promise A Safe Landing.

— Compiled by Michael Burdette

Jesus Prevails When All Else Fails.

– Compiled by Michael Burdette

~ Lessons At The Cross ~

Patience Is A Virtue Which Carries A Lot Of Wait.

– Compiled by Michael Burdette

The Cost Of Obedience Is Nothing Compared To The Cost Of Disobedience.

– Compiled by Michael Burdette

~ Lessons At The Cross ~

~ Lessons At The Cross ~

Feed Your Faith ... It Will Starve Your Doubts.

– Compiled by Michael Burdette

God Did Not Give You The Spirit Of Fear ... He Gave You The Spirit Of Power.

– Compiled by Michael Burdette

~ Lessons At The Cross ~

~ Lessons At The Cross ~

Failure Is Never Final For Those Who Begin Again With God.

– Compiled by Michael Burdette

If You Adore Christ As Savior ... You Can't Ignore Christ As Lord.

– Compiled by Michael Burdette

~ Lessons At The Cross ~

Make Sure Your Fruit For Christ Is Not Full Of Sour Grapes.

– Compiled by Michael Burdette

Nails Could Not Have Kept Jesus On The Cross... If His Love For Us Had Not Held Him There.

– Compiled by Michael Burdette

~ Lessons At The Cross ~

When You Come To The Cross Roads In Your Life ... Choose The Road To The Cross.

– Compiled by Michael Burdette

C hrist
R esponse
O n
S aving
S ouls

– Compiled by Michael Burdette

~ Lessons At The Cross ~

~ Lessons At The Cross ~

Our Greatest Weakness May Be Our Failure Not To Rely On God's Strength.

– Compiled by Michael Burdette

Milk Does A Body Good!
Christ Does Everybody Good!

– Compiled by Michael Burdette

~ Lessons At The Cross ~

When Jesus Christ My Savior Suffered Loss ... It Was My Sin That Nailed Him To The Cross.

– Compiled by Michael Burdette

The World Functions By Vision ... God's People Live By Revelation.

– Compiled by Michael Burdette

Vision Is Something People Produce ... Revelation Is Something People Receive.

– Compiled by Michael Burdette

To Know Your Life's Purpose, You Must First Know Your Life's Creator.

– Compiled by Michael Burdette

Success In Marriage Is Not Finding The Right Person But Becoming The Right Person.

– Compiled by Michael Burdette

To Live For Christ ... We Must Die To Self.

– Compiled by Michael Burdette

~ Lessons At The Cross ~

Our Day's Work Isn't Done Until We Build Up Someone.

– Compiled by Michael Burdette

Jesus Is The Only Fountain Who Can Satisfy The Thirsty Soul.

– Compiled by Michael Burdette

~ Lessons At The Cross ~

The Spirit Of God Uses The Word Of God To Change The People Of God.

– Compiled by Michael Burdette

No Christ ... No Peace; Know Christ ... Know Peace.

– Compiled by Michael Burdette

~ Lessons At The Cross ~

~ Lessons At The Cross ~

A Christian On Fire For God Can Stop People Being Burned By Satan.

– Compiled by Michael Burdette

Give Christ The Keys ... He Will Unlock All The Doors.

– Compiled by Michael Burdette

~ Lessons At The Cross ~

~ Lessons At The Cross ~

Hold Loosely To Things That Are Temporal And Tightly To Things That Are Eternal.

– Compiled by Michael Burdette

Because The Tomb Was Empty ... Your Heart Can Be Filled.

– Compiled by Michael Burdette

~ Lessons At The Cross ~

~ Lessons At The Cross ~

**In The Drama Of Life ...
God Is The Director Behind
The Scenes.**

– Compiled by Michael Burdette

The Bible Is Meant To Be Bread For Daily Use ... Not Cake For A Special Occasion.

– Compiled by Michael Burdette

When Life Is Filled With Shadows ... Face The Sunshine Of God's Love.

– Compiled by Michael Burdette

**Worship God On Sunday ...
Then Walk With Him
On Monday.**

– Compiled by Michael Burdette

~ Lessons At The Cross ~

~ Lessons At The Cross ~

**For A Christ-Like Walk ...
Keep In Step With Christ.**

— Compiled by Michael Burdette

Don't Be Just Informed About Christ ... Let Him Transform You As Well.

– Compiled by Michael Burdette

~ Lessons At The Cross ~

**Give Your All For Jesus ...
He Gave His All For You.**

– Compiled by Michael Burdette

Christ Paid A Debt He Didn't Owe To Cancel A Debt We Couldn't Pay.

– Compiled by Michael Burdette

~ Lessons At The Cross ~

~ Lessons At The Cross ~

The Flowers Or Weeds That Spring Up Tomorrow Are In The Seeds We Sow Today.

– Compiled by Michael Burdette

We Don't Need More To Be Thankful For ... We Just Need To Be More Thankful.

– Compiled by Michael Burdette

~ Lessons At The Cross ~

~ Lessons At The Cross ~

Revenge Gets You Even With Your Enemy ... Forgiveness Puts You Above Him.

– Compiled by Michael Burdette

Your Life Will Either Shed Light Or Cast A Shadow.

– Compiled by Michael Burdette

~ Lessons At The Cross ~

God Can Bring Showers Of Blessing Out Of Storms Of Turmoil.

– Compiled by Michael Burdette

Those Who Are Prepared To Die Are Prepared To Live.

– Compiled by Michael Burdette

~ Lessons At The Cross ~

~ Lessons At The Cross ~

When It's Time To Die ... Make Sure That's All You Have To Do.

– Compiled by Michael Burdette

When You Can't See God's Hand ... Trust His Heart.

– Compiled by Michael Burdette

~ Lessons At The Cross ~

~ Lessons At The Cross ~

**Once You Face Your Sins ...
You Can Then Put Them
Behind You.**

– Compiled by Michael Burdette

Salvation Is Free ... But The Price Was High.

– Compiled by Michael Burdette

~ Lessons At The Cross ~

You Cannot Bear Good Fruit Without The Water Of God's Word.

– Compiled by Michael Burdette

You Can Live In The World ...
But Don't Let The World
Live In You.

— Compiled by Michael Burdette

~ Lessons At The Cross ~

If You Don't Hold Your Tongue ... You May Have To Eat Your Words.

– Compiled by Michael Burdette

You Will Be Able To Trust The Bible When You Get To Know The Author.

– Compiled by Michael Burdette

~ Lessons At The Cross ~

The Symbol Of Our Christian Faith Is A Cross ... Not An Easy Chair ... Get Up.

– Compiled by Michael Burdette

Death Is The Last Chapter Of Time But The First Chapter Of Eternity.

– Compiled by Michael Burdette

~ Lessons At The Cross ~

None Are So Poor As Those Whose Only Wealth Is Money.

– Compiled by Michael Burdette

Stop Showing Forgiveness To Others When God Stops Showing His To You.

– Compiled by Michael Burdette

~ Lessons At The Cross ~

The Time To Make Friends Is Before You Need Them.

– Compiled by Michael Burdette

We Are Judged By How We Finish ... Not By How We Start.

– Compiled by Michael Burdette

~ Lessons At The Cross ~

To Master The Keys To Success ... You Must Know The Master.

– Compiled by Michael Burdette

**Many Books Will Inform ...
Only The Bible Can
Transform.**

– Compiled by Michael Burdette

~ Lessons At The Cross ~

~ Lessons At The Cross ~

Jesus Christ Is Your Upgrade To First Class.

– Compiled by Michael Burdette

Always Look At Others Through The Eyes Of Christ ... It's Always A Better View.

– Compiled by Michael Burdette

Uproot The Weeds Of Sin Before They Choke The Whole Garden.

– Compiled by Michael Burdette

When The World Couldn't Care Less ... We Need To Care More.

– Compiled by Michael Burdette

~ Lessons At The Cross ~

When You Sing Your Own Praise ... You Will Always Be Out Of Tune.

– Compiled by Michael Burdette

God Takes Us Into The Darkroom To Develop Our Character.

– Compiled by Michael Burdette

~ Lessons At The Cross ~

~ Lessons At The Cross ~

Pride Is The First Brick That Builds A Wall Between You And God.

– Compiled by Michael Burdette

To Build A Godly Life ... Let God Be The Architect And His Word The Blueprints.

– Compiled by Michael Burdette

~ Lessons At The Cross ~

~ Lessons At The Cross ~

To Find Your Way To Salvation ... You Must First Admit You're Lost.

– Compiled by Michael Burdette

God Is Strong ... Big And Tall ... But He's One Size That Fits All.

– Compiled by Michael Burdette

~ Lessons At The Cross ~

~ Lessons At The Cross ~

Sin Builds Up Walls ... Jesus Brings Them Down.

– Compiled by Michael Burdette

**The Man With The Most Toys
When He Dies Still Dies ...
Win With The Lord.**

– Compiled by Michael Burdette

~ Lessons At The Cross ~

~ Lessons At The Cross ~

We Must Adjust Our Lives To The Bible ... Never The Bible To Our Lives.

– Compiled by Michael Burdette

As You Go Through Life ... Concentrate On The Roses Instead Of The Thorns.

– Compiled by Michael Burdette

~ Lessons At The Cross ~

God's Delays Are Not God's Denials.

– Compiled by Michael Burdette

God Will Never Demolish You ... Instead He Will Always Polish You.

– Compiled by Michael Burdette

~ Lessons At The Cross ~

You Don't Polish A Stone With A Feather.

– Compiled by Michael Burdette

To Handle Life's Frictions ... Start With God's Addictions.

– Compiled by Michael Burdette

Live Your Life With An Attitude Of Gratitude.

– Compiled by Michael Burdette

To Ease Another's Burden ...
Help Him Carry It.

– Compiled by Michael Burdette

~ Lessons At The Cross ~

When You Taste God's Goodness ... His Praise Will Be On Your Lips.

– Compiled by Michael Burdette

You Can't Find The Highway To Heaven If You Bypass Jesus.

– Compiled by Michael Burdette

~ Lessons At The Cross ~

~ Lessons At The Cross ~

Following Jesus Is Always Right ... But Not Always Easy.

– Compiled by Michael Burdette

**Unless We're Humble ...
We're Sure To Stumble.**

– Compiled by Michael Burdette

~ Lessons At The Cross ~

In Every Desert Of Pain ... God Has An Oasis Of Grace.

– Compiled by Michael Burdette

Open Your Ears To God Before You Open Your Mouth To Others.

– Compiled by Michael Burdette

The World's Crown Of Success Holds No Shine Compared To God's Crown Of Faithfulness.

– Compiled by Michael Burdette

All Christians Have The Same Employer ... They Just Have Different Jobs.

– Compiled by Michael Burdette

~ Lessons At The Cross ~

~ Lessons At The Cross ~

All We Own Is Really On Loan.

– Compiled by Michael Burdette

God Has Not Promised To Keep Us From Life's Storms ... But To Help Us Navigate Them.

– Compiled by Michael Burdette

~ Lessons At The Cross ~

We Are Saved By God's Mercy ... Not Our Merits; By Christ Dying ... Not By Our Doing.

– Compiled by Michael Burdette

Coincidence Is God's Way Of Staying Anonymous.

– Compiled by Michael Burdette

~ Lessons At The Cross ~

~ Lessons At The Cross ~

You Will Never Fall For What's Wrong If You Always Stand For What's Right.

– Compiled by Michael Burdette

**To Master Life ... Give Your Life To The Master.
Give God A Try ... If You Don't Like It, The Devil Will Always Take You Back.**

– Compiled by Michael Burdette

~ Lessons At The Cross ~

~ Lessons At The Cross ~

**To Rise Above Temptation ...
Just Reach A Little Higher
To God.**

– Compiled by Michael Burdette

A Lie May Cover Your Tracks ... But The Truth Will Eventually Derail You.

— Compiled by Michael Burdette

To Break Sin's Grip ...
Put Yourself In God's Hands.

– Compiled by Michael Burdette

~ Lessons At The Cross ~

In The Light Of Christ's Brilliance ... The World's Wisdom Is But A Shadow.

– Compiled by Michael Burdette

~ Lessons At The Cross ~

Deposit God's Word Daily In Your Memory Bank ... You'll Draw Interest For Life.

– Compiled by Michael Burdette

True Faith Produces A Life Full Of Actions ... Not A Head Full Of Facts.

– Compiled by Michael Burdette

~ Lessons At The Cross ~

A Steady Diet Of God's Word Will Keep You Growing And You'll Never Be Full.

– Compiled by Michael Burdette

The Cross Of Christ Reveals God's Love At Its Best and Man's Sin At Its Worst.

– Compiled by Michael Burdette

~ Lessons At The Cross ~

~ Lessons At The Cross ~

The Good News Is Not That Jesus Lived And Died ... But That He Died And Lives.

– Compiled by Michael Burdette

We Have The Power Of Free Will Because Christ Paid The Price.

– Compiled by Michael Burdette

~ Lessons At The Cross ~

Lessons At The Cross

When You're Green With Envy ... You're Ripe For Trouble.

– Compiled by Michael Burdette

Adding Up Your Blessings Will Multiply Your Joy.

– Compiled by Michael Burdette

~ Lessons At The Cross ~

~ Lessons At The Cross ~

If You're Too Busy To Pray ... You're Too Busy.

– Compiled by Michael Burdette

The Easiest Way To Tell People What Christ Can Do For Them Is To Tell Them What Christ Has Done For You.

– Compiled by Michael Burdette

~ Lessons At The Cross ~

When All You Have Is God ...
You Have All You Need.

– Compiled by Michael Burdette

The Best Reason For Doing What's Right Today Is Tomorrow.

– Compiled by Michael Burdette

~ Lessons At The Cross ~

~ Lessons At The Cross ~

In God's Eyes ... It Is A Great Thing To Do A Little Thing Well.

– Compiled by Michael Burdette

God Uses Life's Stops To Prepare Us For The Next Start.

— Compiled by Michael Burdette

~ Lessons At The Cross ~

Lessons At The Cross

When God Is In Your Pit Crew ... He Will Get You Back On Track.

– Compiled by Michael Burdette

**Prayer Is The Soil In Which
Hope And Healing
Grow Best.**

– Compiled by Michael Burdette

~ Lessons At The Cross ~

P ray
U until
S omething
H appens.

– Compiled by Michael Burdette

If We Pause To Think ... We'll Find Cause To Thank.

– Compiled by Michael Burdette

~ Lessons At The Cross ~

Lessons At The Cross

God – Who Knows Our Load Limit – Graciously Limits Our Load.

– Compiled by Michael Burdette

We Stumble Over Pebbles ...
Not Mountains.

– Compiled by Michael Burdette

God Calls Us To Get Into The Game ... Not To Keep Score.

– Compiled by Michael Burdette

You Are Heading In The Right Direction When You Walk With God.

– Compiled by Michael Burdette

~ Lessons At The Cross ~

~ Lessons At The Cross ~

If You Think You Know Everything ... You've Got A Lot To Learn.

– Compiled by Michael Burdette

Gems Of Truth Are Found In The Bible ... But You Must Dig For Them.

– Compiled by Michael Burdette

~ Lessons At The Cross ~

No One Is Good Enough To Save Himself … No One Is So Bad That God Cannot Save Him.

– Compiled by Michael Burdette

**Contentment Comes Not
From Great Wealth ...
But From Few Wants.**

– Compiled by Michael Burdette

~ Lessons At The Cross ~

Life On Earth Is A Temporary Assignment ... Christ Prepares Us For Our Permanent Job.

– Compiled by Michael Burdette

Uplift Your Heart ... By Downloading Christ Into It.

– Compiled by Michael Burdette

~ Lessons At The Cross ~

You Will Never Stumble When You're On Your Knees.

– Compiled by Michael Burdette

Life On Earth Is Just A Dress Rehearsal Before The Real Production.

– Compiled by Michael Burdette

~ Lessons At The Cross ~

**Honesty Means You Never
Have To Look Over
Your Shoulder.**

– Compiled by Michael Burdette

God May Conceal The Purpose Of His Ways ... But His Ways Are Not Without Purpose.

— Compiled by Michael Burdette

~ Lessons At The Cross ~

Lessons At The Cross

Wisdom Is Knowing When To Speak Your Mind And When To Mind Your Speech.

– Compiled by Michael Burdette

You Can't Store Up Treasures In Heaven If You're Holding On To The Treasures Of Earth.

– Compiled by Michael Burdette

~ Lessons At The Cross ~

~ Lessons At The Cross ~

Marriages May Be Made In Heaven ... But They Have To Be Worked Out On Earth.

– Compiled by Michael Burdette

**To Silence Gossip ...
Refuse To Repeat It.**

— Compiled by Michael Burdette

~ Lessons At The Cross ~

God Will Give You Strength In Proportion To The Strain.

– Compiled by Michael Burdette

**The Soul Would Have No
Rainbow If The Eyes
Had No Tears.**

– Compiled by Michael Burdette

~ Lessons At The Cross ~

He Who Waits On The Lord Will Not Be Crushed By The Weight Of Adversity.

– Compiled by Michael Burdette

The Bible Is A Mirror That Lets Us See Ourselves As God Sees Us.

– Compiled by Michael Burdette

~ Lessons At The Cross ~

~ Lessons At The Cross ~

Sin Always Makes The Grass Look Greener Until You Realize It's Astro Turf.

– Compiled by Michael Burdette

Master Your Habits Or Your Habits Will Master You.

— Compiled by Michael Burdette

~ Lessons At The Cross ~

~ Lessons At The Cross ~

You Will Be Content When You Want God's Will More Than You Want Your Way.

– Compiled by Michael Burdette

The Smallest Of Deeds Are Greater Than The Biggest Intentions.

– Compiled by Michael Burdette

You May Give Without Loving ... But You'll Never Love Without Giving.

– Compiled by Michael Burdette

The Lord Not Only Sees What We Give ... But Also What We Keep.

– Compiled by Michael Burdette

~ Lessons At The Cross ~

~ Lessons At The Cross ~

Those Who Deserve Love The Least ... Need It The Most.

– Compiled by Michael Burdette

**Faith Doesn't Stand Around
Idle With Its Hands In
Its Pockets.**

– Compiled by Michael Burdette

~ Lessons At The Cross ~

If You Don't Stand For God ... You'll Fall For Anything.

– Compiled by Michael Burdette

When You Feed On God's Truth ... It Keeps You From Swallowing The World's Lies.

– Compiled by Michael Burdette

~ Lessons At The Cross ~

~ Lessons At The Cross ~

When You See People Without A Smile ... Just Give Them One Of Yours.

– Compiled by Michael Burdette

**Faith In Christ Enables Us
To Live Above Our
Circumstances ...
Not Under Them.**

– Compiled by Michael Burdette

~ Lessons At The Cross ~

When You Are Swept Off Your Feet ... Land On Your Knees.

– Compiled by Michael Burdette

To Be Spiritually Fruitful ...
Plant God's Word In
Your Heart.

– Compiled by Michael Burdette

~ Lessons At The Cross ~

~ Lessons At The Cross ~

The Richest People I Know On Earth Are The Ones Who Invest Their Lives In Heaven.

– Compiled by Michael Burdette

**Compassion Never
Goes Out Of Fashion.**

– Compiled by Michael Burdette

A Thirst For God Can Only Be Satisfied By Christ, The Living Water.

– Compiled by Michael Burdette

What We Practice Is The Best Illustration Of What We Preach.

– Compiled by Michael Burdette

Evangelism Is Nothing More Than One Beggar Telling Another Beggar Where To Find Bread.

– Compiled by Michael Burdette

If God Had A Refrigerator ... Your Picture Would Be On It.

– Compiled by Michael Burdette

~ Lessons At The Cross ~

~ Lessons At The Cross ~

Never Take On More Things Than You Have Time To Pray About.

– Compiled by Michael Burdette

**Make Prayer Your
First Response ...
Not Your Last Resort.**

– Compiled by Michael Burdette

~ Lessons At The Cross ~

~ Lessons At The Cross ~

The Pathway To Heaven Starts At The Foot Of The Cross.

– Compiled by Michael Burdette

To Stay Spiritually Fit ... Work Out Daily With The Lord.

– Compiled by Michael Burdette

~ Lessons At The Cross ~

~ Lessons At The Cross ~

**Faith Is More Than Believing
Christ Can Save …
It's Asking Him To Do It.**

– Compiled by Michael Burdette

When You're Unable To Fall Asleep ... Don't Count Sheep ... Talk To The Shepherd.

– Compiled by Michael Burdette

~ Lessons At The Cross ~

~ Lessons At The Cross ~

When You Know God's Hand Is In Everything ... You Can Leave Everything In God's Hands.

– Compiled by Michael Burdette

God Chooses What We Go Through ... We Choose How We Go Through It.

– Compiled by Michael Burdette

~ Lessons At The Cross ~

~ Lessons At The Cross ~

You'll Find The Courage To Stand When You Kneel Before The Lord.

– Compiled by Michael Burdette

Life Is Like A Game Of Tennis ... You Can't Win Without Serving Well.

– Compiled by Michael Burdette

~ Lessons At The Cross ~

Success Means That You Get Up One More Time Than You Fall Down.

– Compiled by Michael Burdette

Worry Will Never Improve The Future ... It Only Ruins The Present.

– Compiled by Michael Burdette

~ Lessons At The Cross ~

~ Lessons At The Cross ~

Salvation Is A Gift To Be Received ... Not A Goal To Be Achieved.

– Compiled by Michael Burdette

When You Flee Temptation ... Be Sure You Don't Leave A Forwarding Address.

– Compiled by Michael Burdette

~ Lessons At The Cross ~

Most Often ... Falling Into Sin Is Not A Blowout, But More Of A Slow Leak.

– Compiled by Michael Burdette

Life's Trials Should Make Us Better ... Not Bitter.

~

The Tongue Is A Small Organ That Creates Either Discord Or Harmony.

– Compiled by Michael Burdette

~ Lessons At The Cross ~

May The God Of Hope Fill You With Joy And Peace In Believing, That You May Abound In Hope By The Power Of The Holy Spirit.

-Romans 15:13

– Compiled by Michael Burdette